JESUS IS BORN

This Bible story is found in Luke 1, 2; Matthew 1:18-25.

illustrated by John A. Nelson

A CANDLE BOOK Printed and bound in Italy for Send The Light
Coedition arranged with Angus Hudson, London
© 1980 The STANDARD PUBLISHING Company, Cincinnati, Ohio

A long, long time ago God told His prophets about a special baby who would be born. He would be God's Son.

Many years later, God sent His angel Gabriel to Mary.

The angel told Mary that she would have a baby boy.
He would be God's Son.
And she should name Him Jesus.

Mary was engaged to a man named Joseph.

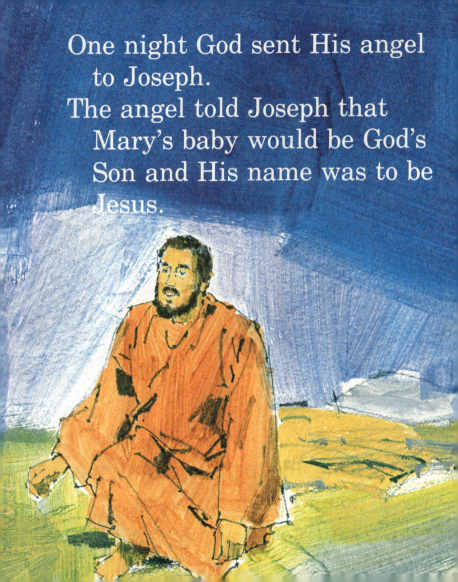

One night God sent His angel to Joseph.
The angel told Joseph that Mary's baby would be God's Son and His name was to be Jesus.

Mary and Joseph were married. They lived in the town of Nazareth.

One day a soldier from the king came to tell of a new law. Everyone had to go to a town and sign his name.

Mary and Joseph had to go to
   Bethlehem.
It was a long trip.

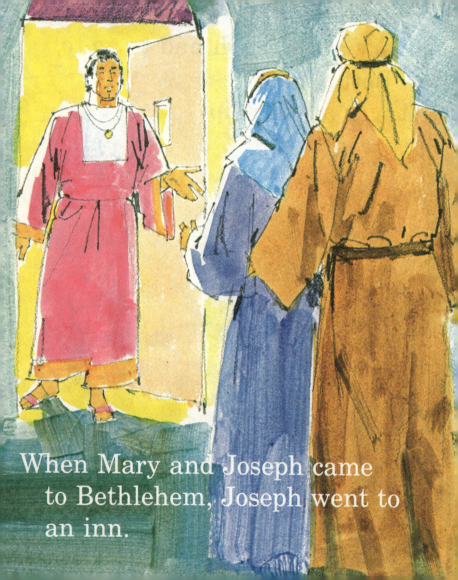

When Mary and Joseph came to Bethlehem, Joseph went to an inn.

He knocked on the door.
The innkeeper shook his head.
There was no room.
"But you can stay in the stable," he said.

So Mary and Joseph stayed in the stable.

That night something wonderful happened!
The baby God had promised was born.

Mary wrapped the baby in a soft cloth and laid Him in a manger.
Mary and Joseph remembered what the angel had said.
They named the baby Jesus.

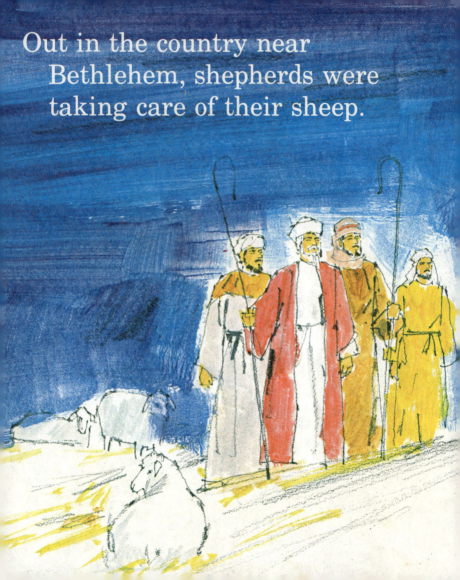
Out in the country near Bethlehem, shepherds were taking care of their sheep.

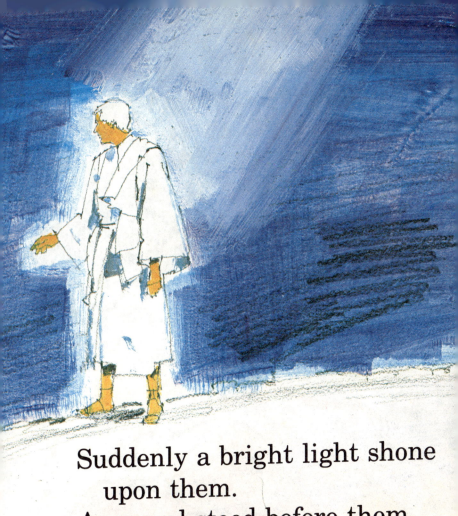

Suddenly a bright light shone upon them.
An angel stood before them.

The angel said,
"Do not be afraid.
I have good news.
Tonight in Bethlehem, God's
 Son was born.
His name is Jesus.
You will find Him wrapped
 in cloths.
He is lying in a manger."

Then there were many angels.

They said, "Glory to God in the highest. And on earth, peace and goodwill to men."

Then the angels were gone.
The sky was dark.

The shepherds said, "Let's go and see this baby!"

The shepherds went to the stable.

They found Mary and Joseph, and the baby lying in a manger.

As the shepherds went home, they thanked God for sending His Son, Jesus.